Contents

3 From the Desk of the President

7 What the Rich Know (and You Need to Know)

13 Hyper-Efficient Social Media Marketing

19 Start with Vision

27 Starting a Local Community Business

31 Managing Diversity and Change

36 Pilates for Everyone

39 CBD School

43 How to Build a Successful Product Brand

I0048415

On the cover: Will Black, CEO of Sharing the Credit and Director of Finance, Strategic Advisor Board. See our story on page 7.

From the Editor

In this issue, I'm delighted to introduce you to Will Black. Will's company, Sharing The Credit, has not only saved business owners millions of dollars in credit card fees, but has also helped those same business owners and their customers give millions of dollars to their favorite charities.

Jared Dalton was awarded the prestigious Nashville Black 40 under 40 award. He shares social media marketing secrets that will explode your business.

Tony DUrso, a podcasting giant, shares his Vision Map™ process with us. His podcast, The Tony DUrso show, has over 30 million downloads and is the #1 podcast on Chartable worldwide.

Amy Blain is a community expert. She explains how to start your own local community-based business online. Her winning website is ExplorePeoria.com.

Joe Trujillo, one of the ten directors of the Strategic Advisor Board, teaches us how to manage diversity and change in the workplace.

Meirav Cohen reveals how Pilates is for everyone, not only those who are already fit.

Melanie Kossan explains the inner workings of a CBD business and shares some unique business models.

PIVOT Magazine

Founder and President
Jason Miller
jason@strategicadvisorboard.com

Editor-in-Chief
Chris O'Byrne
chris@jetlaunch.net

Advertising
Chris O'Byrne
chris@jetlaunch.net

Webmaster
Joel Phillips
joel@proshark.com

Editor
Laura West
laura@jetlaunch.net

Cover Design
Debbie O'Byrne

Jason is a seasoned CEO with an overwhelming passion for helping other business owners and CEOs succeed. He was nicknamed "The Bull" because he takes no BS and no excuses from the people he serves. He has mentored thousands of people for over 20 years. Jason's major strengths are in project management, hyper-company-growth and scaling, and strategic and operational implementation. Jason has built several companies of his own from the ground up since the late 90s.

Jason's specialty is in helping businesses create a passive system of income and guiding other business owners through the rough waters of growing and scaling their company in sequence.

Jason currently operates the Strategic Advisor Board, Miller & Company, and several other companies with multiple brands, including a full-service marketing agency, a staffing agency, a publishing company, and a government-contracting branch where services can be provided for multiple agencies of the US Government.

Jason is a bestselling author in the business world and has reached international bestseller three times. His seven published books have been featured at Barnes & Noble stores worldwide and are also available on Amazon and most online retailers. Jason donates all his book sales to Homes for Heroes, of which donations have played a part in building multiple homes for the Wounded Warrior Project. Jason has also been featured in *Voyage Denver* magazine twice for being one of Colorado's most inspiring companies. He has also been featured on FORBES, ENTREPRENEUR, ABC, FOX, NBC, CBS, and many more. Jason holds an MBA and continues to educate himself as a lifelong learner.

Jason is also the creator of the famous Strategic Advisor Board podcast, *War Room Round Table*, which is in the top 1.5% of all podcasts worldwide, where he and his co-host, the prior host of *Entrepreneur* and *Inc. Magazine*'s podcasts, talk about business and how we leave a footprint.

Jason and his wife also spent a combined twenty-five years in the service to their country in the United States Army while simultaneously growing and scaling multiple businesses and setting them on autopilot with the correct staffing and systems put in place.

If you need help with hyper-growth and scaling your company in the proper sequence, that's where Jason can assist your company to the next level.

Jason is married to his fabulous wife and is a proud father of four children and a grandpa of three. Jason and his family reside and run their main company headquarters in Boulder, CO, in the stunning Rocky Mountains.

Companies (Brands):

Founder / CEO – Strategic Advisor Board

Founder / Senior Chairman - Miller & Company

Founder / Senior Chairman - Jump Start Marketing Concepts

Founder / Senior Chairman - The Ads Agency

Founder / Senior Chairman - Reliable Staff Solutions

Founder / Senior Chairman - The SOEP Group

Principal / Chairman - Rogue Publishing Partners

President / Principal - PIVOT Magazine

Principal / Chairman - Proshark

Principal / Chairman - Imperium Authority

Principal / Chairman - JETLAUNCH Publishing

Principal / Chairman - Sharing The Credit

JETLAUNCH

WRITE AND PUBLISH YOUR BOOK FAST
THE SOLUTION FOR BUSY ENTREPRENEURS

JETLAUNCH.NET

From the Desk of the President

People ask me all the time why success comes to some so easily, while most struggle to simply survive and earn a living. Obviously, talent and drive factor into the equation, but I've often seen people with average skills become world-shakers despite their ordinary abilities. How do they do it, and what allows them to pull away from the pack?

The keys to success are similar to looking for buried treasure. You know there's a gold mine out there somewhere—the challenge is finding it. Having a map would be a big help, right?

Starting a business and turning it into a market leader and winning more customers than your competitors also requires knowing where you're going and drawing a path to getting there.

In the same way, developing a strategy and then implementing it effectively is essential to building a thriving business.

To make it easy for my clients to remember and follow these imperatives to have focus and determination, I created two acronyms. This goes back to the early part of 2001, and as a guiding light for success, I have never seen it fail. I personally have used them in every company I have owned and insist upon them in the entrepreneurs I work with at the Strategic Advisor Board.

To begin, it takes SPIRIT

Achieving greatness at multiple levels of your endeavors requires having the spirit of an entrepreneur. This is what will get you through the hard times when running your own business. There are no shortcuts, only entrepreneurs who sell themselves short.

Follow these simple tips as you get started and use them as a guide to your success. Write this acronym down and look at it in the morning when you face the day and at night when you think back on the victories and hurdles you experienced.

Self-sufficient and disciplined
Passionate
Integrity
Respected by others
Imagination
Tools for success

Use these principles as your guiding light, and you will always be heading in the right direction in your business:

Be self-sufficient and disciplined in everything you do. Whether it's setting your hours of operations as a business owner or deciding how much family time you want to spend daily, be self-sufficient and disciplined with your choices. You are now accountable to yourself!

Do something you are passionate about. Find your passion in life and work your business and your lifestyle around it. If you are passionate about what you do, then it won't feel like work. It will be fun, and you will enjoy doing it every day. You can also share your passion with your family and make it a family business like my family and I have done.

Always maintain integrity. It's something you can't get back. Once it's gone, it's gone. Be honest with your customers, and don't be afraid to admit that you did something wrong. Mistakes happen in business; own them and move on.

Be respected by others. That means everyone you come into contact with—in your community, with your customers, employees, family, and other leaders in your field. Respect goes a long way with the people that surround you. They are the ones that

will help you take your business to the next level.

Use your imagination. In childhood, our minds are open to everything we take in. That mindset breeds creativity. Many of the legendary business leaders and greatest creative thinkers openly admit they embrace wonderment and allow themselves to view the world through the prism of how they were as a child. Steve Jobs comes to mind, as do Walt Disney, Elon Musk, Frank Gehry, and Steven Spielberg. Some of your best ideas will come with creative thinking and being a dreamer. No idea is too big or too small to try. Be inventive, innovative, and adaptive by letting your imagination take you to new levels. The only unsuccessful idea is the one you never tried!

Get the best tools. Having the right resources and systems at your fingertips is invaluable. When you save time by operating more efficiently, you're creating the foundation for maximum success. Having the right tools, systems, and processes in your business endeavors will allow you to make breakthroughs that you never thought possible.

Having the right SPIRIT to succeed is critical to your success. What else does it take?

To go all the way, you must be a PATRIOT

Equally important to character and how you shape your thinking processes is the ability to operate as a business. You must be the PATRIOT (The Protector) of your own business and business ventures. Know how your business operates from start to finish. Know your products and customers on an intimate level, and you will achieve greatness.

P.A.T. R.I.O.T.

Planning with consistency
Actions that create revenue
Train, mentor, and coach
Reinvent yourself often
Integrate your systems
Operate with consistency
Turn your ideas into profit

Remembering these operational principles will point you in the right direction for managing your business effectively on a day-to-day basis and into a bright future.

Plan with consistency. If you are consistent with your budget, your products, inventory, and customers, you will see success in your operation. Always be planning the next big thing and thinking about how you can tweak your business to net more profit.

Actions that create revenue are crucial to the health of your business. Often business owners get tied up with doing little tasks they can easily outsource or completely do away with altogether. Focus on revenue-generating processes in your business that affect your bottom line in a positive way. Do this every single day! You must learn how to delegate tactical tasks to those employees in the right seats. A great place to start is working with a staffing agency like Reliable Staff Solutions. They can identify the right employee that sits on the right seat on the bus for your company.

Train, mentor, and coach. This is what true leaders do. Do it thoughtfully and across all those you work with, from your employees to the customers you serve. Step up and be the inspirational leader that you are. The world will not automatically brand you as a leader or an expert. You must own it and become it yourself.

Reinvent yourself often. Don't get tied to a specific idea on an emotional level. If it doesn't work, then scrap it and move on. Reinvent yourself again and continue to make forward progress. Being stubborn and married to a failed idea will lead to poor decision-making and will only cause heartache and drive your business into bankruptcy.

Integrate your systems. Developing and using processes are what make your organization efficient and on track. Technology, which standardizes and automates manual or repetitive tasks, is a wonderful thing. Do your homework and ensure that the systems you use will work for your business.

Operate with consistency. Owning a successful business is all about finding what works and then building upon it on a consistent basis. Think of it as shampoo instructions: wash, rinse, and repeat. Find what works and then maintain the consistency required to simply build upon and accelerate the success you have found.

Turn every idea you have into profit. Be a thinker and be inventive with the things that you do. Aspire to remain on the cutting edge in your field and develop new ideas that produce profit. Remember, the greatest ideas in the world have changed all of our lives. On the same note, an idea is useless without execution!

I invite you (no, I *implore* you) to use these two acronyms above as a road map in your business. These simple tips and strategic ways of thinking will assist you in your path to breaking through and taking the needed steps to your own success. If you need support in your business with either creating strategies that help you grow or staffing to help you transition to the next level, we are here to help.

What the Rich Know (and You Need to Know)

Will Black

If you have a business, you take plastic as a form of payment.

Seriously, how much cash do you take in? And accepting checks is like playing Russian Roulette. Credit cards and debit cards, though, are gold. The first thing a business usually does in the modern world is to get their business license and then get their merchant account. The great mistake at that point is thinking they're done.

The most common flaw at this point is worrying solely about the rate you have to pay. That's important, but what if that little credit card machine could be used to drive traffic to your front door?

My wealthiest clients do exactly that.

Here is what the rich know (because I teach them). Every time a customer comes into your store and swipes a card, fees come out. That part you know. Here's what you don't know. It's a collection of fees, and one of those fees does not go to either Visa or MasterCard. It goes back into the system, normally to a bank, but did you know someone can legally redirect it to a charity instead? Let me restate that. Every time a customer uses a card at your business, you could be funding a charity.

Here's what doesn't affect it for all the nay-sayers. It doesn't matter if you have a brick-and-mortar or online store. It doesn't matter if it's a debit card or a credit card. The next thing the trolls pull out is the charity. I don't pick the charity, and Visa/MC have no say, either. You do.

It's automated philanthropy, and please let that sink in. As a business, you have almost no choice but to take plastic from clients. We've established that fact. It's a requirement for businesses in the modern world.

When you take plastic, your business pays fees to Visa/MC for handling that. That means the fees they charge you are unavoidable. If you have to pay Visa/MC, do you want fees going into the system to put a bank president in a new Lexus, or do you want to fund something you believe in?

We have given millions of dollars to various charities, money that formerly went back into the system. That feels good to me, to the charities, and especially the businesses involved. It's often thousands of dollars in donations. I have businesses that support schools, animal shelters, ministries, their church, and just about everything else you can think of.

So, what's your favorite charity? What moves you? What would it mean to you to take the money that usually funds the system and instead fund a no-kill animal shelter, a soup kitchen, or a veteran's suicide prevention group? How would that feel? You pay the fees, you might as well support something you believe in.

But how do you get traffic to your store in the first place?

I met a businesswoman years ago who said, "Will, my work isn't the only thing that inspires me." That has always stuck with me. More traffic means more paying clients. Wealthy people are advertising. They are marketing via publicity, and they are doing it through their charities.

It's an incredible business strategy because they are not getting double the blessings, they are getting triple. How? They are using the same dollars three times. First, they pay Visa/MC. Two, they donate to their charity (from the same money).

And three, their charities continually brag about them online—in newsletters, social media and email—giving them free advertising as the business "with a heart," the business that "walks the walk," "does real good in our community," "stands up for their beliefs," "puts their money where their mouth is," and so on.

Guess where all the fans of that charity shop? They shop at the business that gives. After all, they are a fan of that charity, too, so if they have to spend money, they will spend it at a business that shares percentages with their charity.

Let's take a real-world example. The third client we ever spoke to was a car dealership referred to us by the charity themselves. It was a good move. The dealership is not small. In fact, they did $1,000,000 a month in credit card and debit card sales and still do.

They greeted us warmly and asked how we could help them better help their charity. We told them to put on the brakes as we had to get a couple of ground rules down: 1) If this cost the charity anything, or 2) if the car dealership had to pay extra (a premium) in order to do this, it would literally be cheaper to say, "No, thank you."

Their exact words were, "God bless you. We thought you would need a check at the end. Nobody turns away money from us. We're the name in the community." That's when we got to work. We reviewed their statements for the $1,000,000 a month they were doing in plastic sales and came back with, "You're overpaying $30,000 a year in fees."

That's when the big GM spoke up and said, "Wow. That's a car. That's a whole car."

"Actually, sir, it's a car a year. Every year."

That's when we handed them a copy of the report and told them we don't do low pressure—we do *no* pressure. They could see all the red on the report where they were overpaying. We told them to feel free to take it back to their current provider and argue their rates down.

The GM spoke back up and said, "But they're probably not going to give *our* charity this built-in percentage." That is when we tell them their current group can legally do it, but no, they don't have to and probably won't.

"Can you fix this?" they asked. "Can you do this and give the money to *our* charity?" They had made the decision right there.

We took over their account and cut their costs for accepting debit cards and credit cards at their dealership by $30,000. That's $30,000 every year!

It's good for them. It must be good for the business. They are the ones who will support the charity, but they are in business to be in business. They are not in business to support charity. If they can support the charity they love, *and* if it's a savings in fees

9

for their business, then they move on it. This group saves $30,000 a year off the fees Visa/MC would charge their business for taking plastic, but they give $125,000 a year to their charity.

How many dogs does that save in a no-kill shelter? How many veterans does that provide counseling for that keeps them from committing suicide? How many meals does that provide at the soup kitchen? How many clients come back to that dealership because of their giving? According to their own numbers, they hear about it constantly. Their charity always has them at the top of the list in every social media post, in every newsletter, and on their website. That's called publicity, and you should be a fan of it.

Free publicity is a redundant statement, as it's a public statement. Advertising and marketing cost money. Publicity is free, and their charity constantly publicized this dealership. Their charity always keeps their dealership's name in the public eye and helps to make them a household word.

You've seen the trend. People want to buy from those who do good for the public. In fact, a Cone Communications study shows that people will leave the product they are loyal to and buy the competitor's brand *if* the brand shows they do public good.

Imagine owning a dog and although you normally buy Alpo dog food, Kibbles 'n Bits says that when you buy their dog food, you also donate a free bag of food to a no-kill shelter.

About 80% of consumers jump from Alpo and buy Kibbles. They do this because they were going to buy dog food anyway, and this one helps someone else.

The best thing about this is that you don't have to be a million-dollar-a-month car dealer. You can sell pizzas. Now, I buy my family a pizza every two weeks. If I have to choose between pizzerias, I'm going to go to the one that says, "Buy our pizza, and we'll donate to a homeless shelter." It makes me feel good. It's double-coupon day for the soul. In fact, I am going to frequent that pizza place and recommend it to my friends because they show me that they do good.

As for the charities, we tell them their favorite words ever: unrestricted funds. Unlike grants, they can use these monies any way they need. Staff, insurance, gas for the van, and printer ink—everything is on the table.

But, forget the tons of extra traffic.

Forget your charity bragging about you and your business constantly.

Forget the savings.

Forget that the rich do this on purpose and with great intent.

What would it mean to you as a real, live human being to know that every day you work, you automatically help the cause on this earth you care for most? That you are, in fact, a philanthropist and you have built automatic philanthropy into your business? That you save dogs, feed the homeless, fund schools, or save vets every day you open up for business because you made sure it was built it in?

Your business isn't the only thing that inspires you. What's your cause, and what would that mean to you to give to it forever?

About the Author

Will is steeped in the world of merchant accounts and knows the ins and outs of how businesses suffer headache and financial damage via their companies most needful operation: Getting paid in plastic. He has spent three decades in the industry working with hospitals, the military, and everything from the smallest of start-ups to multimillion-dollar-a-month operations. He regularly cuts through the tape and jargon and shows other CEOs and college business classes how they get over-charged, and how to avoid it.

Will specializes in showing non-profits how they can get massive funding from the businesses that support them already by the redirection of a built-in fee that creates long-term, sustainable funding. He has given away $1,000,000+ and is on the $10,000,000 mission now, and most impressively—all in unrestricted funds.

Will started and runs Sharing The Credit, which works with non-profits and their donor companies, and regularly trains non-profits and their development staff in the secret knowledge of merchant accounts.

Will sits on a number of boards including the Coastal Jail Ministry, his local Rotary, Thrivent, and as a member of the Diaconate of his church. He wrote the book *Paid in Plastic: The Art of the Steal*, which trains business owners how to do a month's worth of math in 30 seconds. He is an Amazon bestselling author, an international bestselling author and has written for several business periodicals and been published in TheArtofManliness.com.

If you need help with cutting costs while donating to your favorite cause with "found" money, Will and his team can get you there.

DOING GOOD IS
GOOD BUSINESS

SHARING THE CREDIT

Your business can give to charity without writing a check. Visit **www.SharingTheCredit.com** and start giving today.

High Profile, High Value: The Secrets of Hyper-Efficient Social Media Marketing

Jared Dalton

Shapard Lumberyard is roughly a forty-five-minute drive from my office in Nashville. When Terrance Blakesleay, the owner of this family-owned construction supply company, first called me, he sounded worried.

"You help businesses with marketing?" he asked.

When I said yes, he blurted, "I own a lumber yard here in Columbia. There are twelve other places folks can go to buy wood within a twenty-mile radius, not including a Home Depot and a Lowe's. Columbia is a small community of just under 40,000. How can I stand out and beat my competition to the punch?"

We met for coffee the next day, and I showed him examples of the work my agency does. I explained why well-orchestrated social media marketing works, regardless of the size of your business or the number of competitors vying for the same customer. Two

years later, Terrance is one of our favorite case studies because he went from what I call a "social media skeptic" to a believer.

His experience is not unusual. In fact, during my many meetings with prospective customers about their marketing needs, I hear the same concerns over and over again:

> How can I raise the profile of my business without going broke buying advertising?
>
> What can I do to communicate the unique value I offer my customers?
>
> My competitors are larger than me—how can I gain an unfair advantage over them?
>
> Is it possible to calculate the return I'm getting on my marketing investment?

As an entrepreneur yourself, perhaps you have many of the same concerns. Before I dive into the most pressing worries that

13

keep business owners up at night, I'd like to let you in on a secret: Even the highest-performing CEOs and executives have doubts.

I know this to be true because I've seen it myself in up-close interactions with super successful people. You probably aren't an exception to this rule either, are you?

While virtually all hyper-driven people are blessed with a surplus of confidence, many of us are perfectionists. That means we're determined to do everything right, every time. Yet, how realistic is that? Don't believe me?

As an entrepreneur, how certain are you that your business is doing social media marketing (SMM) correctly? When I pose this question to business professionals attending my talks, the show of hands is sparse. Around 80% to 90% have significant misgivings about their understanding of social media.

Whenever people are in doubt, that means they are fairly sure they're not executing properly. Earlier, I mentioned some of the worries that keep business owners up at night. Here are the two I hear most frequently:

What am I not doing that I should be doing?

What am I not doing as well as I could be doing?

More than any other aspect of digital marketing, the mysterious art of social media marketing remains the least understood challenge and the most difficult to solve for even the most accomplished entrepreneur. The reasons are many, but before I get into those thorny issues, I'd like to share some of the most effective but little-known secrets that will hyper-charge your social media marketing and put virtually all of your misgivings to rest.

I'm Jared Dalton. Like you, I'm a hardworking visionary and forward-thinking entrepreneur determined to help like-minded business owners prosper. In my case, as the owner of an agency specializing in SMM (social media marketing), my mission is to help my clients reach their full potential as entrepreneurs. My motivations are firmly based on the satisfaction my team at The Jared Dalton Agency and I achieve when we perform beyond our clients' expectations.

In serving our customers, we've been fortunate to receive recognition with a trove of awards and citations. Among them are the Nashville "Black 40 under 40" award (which I share with my team), a Comcast Rise grant, an A+ rating from the BBB, and exemplary testimonials from our valued clients, both here in Nashville and across the country. Through hard work and keeping pace with our fast-moving industry, we've grown from humble beginnings to become the #1 resource for companies looking to outsource their SMM, and to date, have served over 75 clients. And we're just getting started!

Let's talk about SMM best practices

With very few exceptions, just about every entrepreneur I've met has one primary objective when it comes to self-promotion. In a nutshell, they want to increase their profile and position themselves as a thought leader. It makes sense when you think about it because becoming well-known makes it easier to expand your sphere of influence and attract clients.

Equally important, having others view you as an expert in your chosen field and a highly knowledgeable personality fosters trust. It's interesting that entrepreneurs instinctively understand the importance of having a high profile and strong credibility in their quest for success because they are also the keys to hyper-effective social media marketing.

Build a high profile

Before the advent of social media, the options to raise the profile of your business were quite limited. You could advertise on the radio and television, display ads in the newspaper, and maybe hand out fliers at public events. All of these were somewhat expensive and only created a one-way dialog. With the rise of the World Wide Web in 1994, the marketing landscape began to shift gradually. The internet, as they say, changed everything.

First came banner ads, then email marketing, and finally social networks. With the launch of what is considered the first social network, SixDegrees.com, in 1997, and subsequently Friendster, Myspace, LinkedIn, XING, and Facebook, a new world of promotional possibilities opened up. Not only can you reach more people with much less spending than traditional print and broadcast media using SMM, but it gives you the power of real-time interaction with your audience.

Engaging in a two-way dialog with your clients and prospects is a perpetual selling opportunity. Ongoing selling potential is why it is crucial to ensure you continually raise your profile and enhance your social network presence.

In building your profile, consider your personality and how you want your audience to perceive you. The more well-defined your tone and voice, the greater the emotional response you will create. *Effective engagement* with your connections effectively creates trust and respect. Depending on your business, it may make sense to position your business brand as synonymous with your profile.

Many of the most successful and well-known personalities *are* their brand. Oprah Winfrey is possibly the most high-profile (and wealthiest) example of this approach. As her fame grew from her daily talk show, she applied her O brand to a variety of products: Oprah magazine, cable network Oxygen, Oprah's Book Club, ready-to-eat meals (O, That's Good! in partnership with Kraft Heinz), and even Weight Watchers (WW) when she became a minority shareholder.

Other famous personalities inextricably linked to their brands include Martha Stewart, Tony Robbins, Kathy Ireland, Coco Chanel, Ralph Lauren, Elon Musk, Giorgio Armani, Mark Cuban, and many more. In 1997, social psychologist Jennifer Aaker defined the Five Dimension Model of the most common (and presumably most powerful) brand personalities:

Excitement: Carefree, spirited, and youthful

Sincerity: Kindness, thoughtfulness, and an orientation toward family values

Ruggedness: Rough, tough, outdoorsy, and athletic

Competence: Successful, accomplished, and influential, highlighted by leadership

Sophistication: Elegant, prestigious, and sometimes even pretentious

While not all these emotion-based profiles will apply to the image you want to project, this list provides a valuable backdrop for your unique voice and brand. You can adopt one or mix and match according to the needs of your brand and the topics you're addressing in your content.

Deliver high value

When taking on the challenge of establishing your profile, don't neglect to develop content to support the persona you feel will be most effective in capturing the attention and earning the loyalty of your audience. Even the most famous influencer loses momentum and becomes ignored when they do not focus on offering value to their target audience.

So, how does one deliver high value? It all begins with writing, curating, and engaging. That, and posting content consistently to keep your followers coming back, are the key to delivering high value.

Writing is a chore for many of us, which is why The Jared Dalton Agency offers copywriting services to our clients. However, if you write about what you know and enjoy doing, which hopefully is at least a partial focus of your business, it can be easier and become a routine part of your day. Try it, and you might surprise yourself.

Another way to keep your social media and blog posts fresh is to find content from news outlets, trade publications, and other sources, and to post it on your account. Make sure it is relevant to your personality and business and also of substantial interest, or you'll gain few "likes" and probably lose followers.

Also, correctly attribute the source and consider providing a courtesy link to the story's origin. There are ways to automate the process of curating content, such as using software that aggregates RSS feeds and streams articles to your social media accounts.

Various strategies will make your content "stickier," encourage people to share it with others, and draw in more followers. Here are a few ideas:

- Run contests and offer discounts or giveaways
- Post opinion polls to take the pulse of your audience
- Join special-interest groups
- Use high-resolution photos and videos
- Engage with influencers and collaborate with partners and followers
- Inject some humor into your posts (avoid controversial topics such as politics)
- Livestream topics of interest going on in your business and involving team members
- Have a sign-up for a customer loyalty program
- Generate engagement through polls and questions
- Always use hashtags, geotags, and account tagging features offered by the platform

Finally, if you're in the market for a digital marketing agency or already using one, here is a checklist of ongoing initiatives that should serve as the foundation of an effective social marketing program:

Growing your audience
Targeting the right audience with the right content is the key to a successful social media strategy, and it can do wonders in an unbelievably short time.

Increasing your brand awareness
High-value content combined with the proper targeting will capture the attention of potential customers while reminding the public what your brand represents.

Tracking your competitors
You're in a better position to grow and harvest new customers when you have an awareness of what your competitors are messaging on social media and if they are succeeding or failing.

Choosing the best social media platforms
Keeping up with the latest social media trends is a challenging and key aspect of knowing which platforms are appropriate for your business and which are a waste of time and money. For example, the "young" audience that made Facebook the number one platform in the world a decade ago is now better found on TikTok, Instagram, Pinterest, or YouTube.

Targeting your audience and their buying patterns
Capturing the activities, likes, dislikes, and various demographics of your best prospects helps inform the most effective style

of content you should be posting and helps attract new customers.

Building trust

Social media provides a powerful platform to interact with your customers, respond to their queries and complaints, and make your brand a vital part of their lifestyle.

Remember, the goal of delivering high-value content is to position yourself as a thought leader and as a credible source of action-able information. Your objective is to invite the engagement of your followers so that your SMM becomes an anticipated part of their day. It may sound ambitious, but it can be done!

Jared Dalton is a Nashville native and the founder of The Jared Dalton Agency LLC. His agency helps small business owners with their marketing and promotion—most specifically to social media. Jared was awarded with a Nashville Black 40 under 40 award, recipient of Comcast Rise's grant pro-gram, and has an A+ rating with the Better Business Bureau.

Start with Vision

Tony DUrso

Plan to succeed

Is it true that a majority of businesses fail? Multiple studies point to yes. Generally, 75% or more of new businesses utterly fail.

Why?

They did not properly plan to succeed. A piece of paper by itself does not have arms and legs to walk around and do the work. You need something more concrete that will motivate and stimulate you and your team to walk around and do the work.

Sound impossible?

For 75% or more failed businesses, it is. But now, with the Vision Map™, you can propel yourself and your team to succeed more easily. The map helps you do the work; it's self-motivating.

You know this: To have a plan to succeed, you have to plan to succeed. And that includes having a well-thought-out vision.

To give any business a chance, you have to have basic fundamental points in place to launch your business, make it grow, and be successful. A piece of paper just doesn't cut it all by itself.

To have a successful growing business, there are some vital points that you must know: You must have worked them out thoroughly, they must be synchronized with each other, and all employees, consultants, and companies that you depend on must know these items and be in agreement with them if your new business is to meet with a high percentage of success.

Start with vision

The best way to unveil the Vision Map™ is to start off with my own story.

In the fall of 2015, I looked for something I could control myself. I had been an entrepreneur, on and off, for a great many years, and like the events of 2020 and 2021, I found that there were times I could not control my business as well as I wanted.

I found out the hard way that there were often events, protocols, regulations, and mandates that changed the business landscape on an overnight basis.

In seven years as the owner of my own lead generation company, there were four major events that seriously impacted my business and took it down to its knees. Each time, I pulled it back up and grew it well until the next new mandate came along.

Finally, after the 4th new protocol came down the line and impacted my business once again, I decided not to build it back up. I was highly frustrated and looked for what new business I could conquer and better control.

For that matter, how can you be assured of success for any activity you are in charge of, whether it is new or a startup? How can you guarantee the next activity will be a success?

I had to have maximum control over my next business and make it as "government-proof" as possible.

There is a current saying about making a business recession-proof, meaning to have a good business that can withstand a troubled economy.

In my case, I needed something that would not sink, no matter what tsunamis were sent to my industry by governmental actions.

I heard the word "podcast" and looked into it. It seemed to fit what I wanted, so I read everything I could find about it, including a free class, which took a few weeks.

I was a university graduate at this time and had taken many classes, in and out of school (summa cum laude out of LaVerne University, CA), on how to create and establish a business.

(I read more material and books outside of classes, well beyond any established syllabuses at the time.)

As I always like to "zone in" on any activity by diving feet first, I established a "learn as I go" methodology on any endeavor in life, which usually served me faithfully, as it beats the conundrum of the chicken and the egg.

Meaning, how do you get experience if you have to learn first, and how do you learn without getting experience?

I was always a proponent of on-the-job training, feeling it's not worth studying anything, all by itself, without getting your hands wet at the same time.

Work out your map

I read *Beach Money* by Jordan Adler and fortified myself on the power of creating a solid vision before a heavy involvement of time and money in any endeavor of any kind.

What is a vision?

The dictionary states that a vision is the ability to think about or plan the future with imagination or wisdom.

I worked out my own vision and realized it was incomplete on its own. A vision by itself does not get anything done.

Your vision statement tells people what your company wants to actually do, not be. This is like a child telling people what he or she wants to be and do when grown up. That is a good analogy for the vision statement.

But by itself, it is nothing. By itself, it means nothing. By itself, you can be assured of business failure. Do you know any child at all that actually and literally became what the child stated when very young?

I then worked out the rest of the steps needed to accomplish that first item: The Vision. I worked out the Vision Map™ and began to use it on my own new business: podcasting.

I started my *Revenue Chat Radio* podcast with zero guests and zero audience. I was new to the industry, and I did not know any of my guests beforehand. I started podcasting with a one-hour weekly live show in the fall of 2015.

Following the steps of my own Vision Map™ and using the power of social media, I began reaching out and soon started meeting and interviewing experts, bestselling authors, and CEOs who shared their wisdom, advice, and guidance with the world.

Using everything I knew about promoting and getting people's attention, I promoted my own show, acquiring many 1,000s of plays and downloads in the first year.

I realized early on that my own vision was another way to say what I saw myself doing in the future.

A good vision statement requires several well-thought-out, well-crafted items that can take hours and even days to construct.

A good vision statement is the beginning of your success. Consider it like a dream, where you can sit back and imagine your future with whatever you want to imagine. And then commit that to paper.

Establish your purpose

My own purpose of helping startups and entrepreneurs was strong. I hit the proverbial nail on the head on my own reason for podcasting. I found that my purpose was who I was really being.

The dictionary defines purpose as the reason for which something is done or created.

Purpose is why you are doing what you are doing. Purpose is why you want to accomplish something in the future. It is not a goal or objective. It is the reason you go after your goal or objective.

You may be familiar with the word Purpose as a "Mission Statement." That is close. The mission statement often includes the Long-Term Objective (future goal), but it is a separate item.

Your purpose is usually to do or accomplish something. It is your reason for doing it. It is what drives you. It is why you get up every day ready to take on the world. It is why you originally worked on your business or startup without any cash in hand; you did it because you loved it. That's purpose.

While purpose fuels the vision, the vision has to come first because you have to focus on what you really want to do in your life or business. It works to list out vision first and then list Purpose on your Vision Map™ as the second item.

By early 2017 (1½ years after starting), I signed with a major internet radio network (VoiceAmerica) and grew to 50,000 social media followers. My new book, *Elite Entrepreneurs*, became a flash bestseller, with proceeds going to charity.

Establish your long-term objective

Objective means the thing aimed for in your goal. A goal is the object of a person's ambition or effort, the aim or desired result.

You hear of a goal, and that can be miscon-strued, so for our purposes, we are speaking of a long-term accomplishment (a few years maximum).

It is those who think way down the line, far ahead in the future, who accomplish bigger objectives than those who only look ahead a few months.

A century ago, businesses used to have ten, fifteen, and even twenty-year goals. Imagine that?

Today, things move so fast that you can become a millionaire in a day, if not faster. With the right tech in place, the sky is the limit.

The Long-Term Objective is what you are having, what you accomplished, and what's in your hand or on your computer as a completed product or service.

This is not money. Money is the result of having accomplished what you accomplished. That may be a mistake that is made by the majority of startups. You never go after money. You go after producing a product or service that can be utilized by a great number of people.

By the fall of 2017, I hit 1,000,000 downloads and was the number one show on the VoiceAmerica Influencers Channel.

Develop a master plan

A plan is a detailed proposal for doing or achieving something.

A Master Plan, in our sense, means a group of individual actions that you need to take to accomplish your Long-Term Objective (like a giant to-do list stretching out over the years).

The Master Plan covers what you are going to accomplish over the years and is written in the way of accomplishing major items.

For example, if the Master Plan is to get your degree and then open up your own business, the Master Plan lists out the major accomplishments such as the key steps to getting your associate's degree, the key steps to getting your bachelor's degree, and so forth.

There are two parts to the Master Plan detailed just ahead: strategy and tactical.

By the end of 2018, my show had achieved 3,000,000 downloads, and I had made the front cover of *Influential People* magazine.

Work out your strategy

Strategic means your overall aim or plan in accomplishing the Long-Term Objective. The dictionary says, "relating to the identification of long-term or overall aims and interest and the means of achieving them."

The first section of your Master Plan should list out how you are going to accomplish your Long-Term Objective over a period of years. What do you have to do? What do you have to accomplish? What barriers have to be dealt with? How are you going to do that?

Every business is different. Only by rolling up your sleeves and researching will you find out where your competition exists, where your business should exist, and what makes sense for you based on the resources at hand.

By the end of 2019, I achieved 5,000,000 downloads and became the #1 show on the entire VoiceAmerica platform.

Develop a tactical plan

Tactical is relating or constituting actions carefully planned to gain a specific military purpose or advantage.

The second step of your Master Plan should list out those broad Tactical Plan actions that you need to accomplish. In other words, how are you going to take those strategic plan steps and turn them into doable actions that are accomplishable?

Look at the Tactical Plan as a list of things to do that covers years and is written in broad strokes.

By the end of 2020, I achieved 10,000,000 downloads, with social media followers topping 150,000.

Rubber meets the road

There is one key step to put in place after you work out your strategy and Tactical Plan.

Plans are nice, but you have to make money to live, fuel your work, and everything else between. You need to generate income first.

At this point, you have most of the details worked out to launch or grow your business to the next level.

For most startups and entrepreneurs, depending, of course, on a great many factors, it is workable to consider that you should start earning some income between one to three months. Again, this depends on resources available, capital infusion, and a great many items.

With all things considered, you still need proof of concept and workability to attract operating capital.

Thus, it is considered that in thirty to ninety days you should have something that you can start selling and providing to consumers, if at all possible, even if in a crude form.

This step is to work out how you are going to bring in immediate income. If you cannot bring in income within thirty to ninety days, then there is something wrong with the earlier planning steps.

Figure this out. What can you sell or provide immediately to generate income?

Examples:

If you are doing a mastermind group at sea for $10,000 a person, with a plan of at least ten people, then you will need a few months to set that up, right?

If you are doing an online webinar to give information, followed by a pitch to buy your services, then that could take some thirty to sixty days to set up and promote to get in hundreds of people, right?

If you have a simple tech tool idea that you can sell for $9 a month, and get thousands of people using it, then it takes a little time to create and promote it, right?

There is a myriad of examples. The point here is to figure out how you are going to bring in income within the next few months.

If your vision is clear and well worked out, then this step should flow very easily. It may take you days to work out the vision step all on its own. This step is worth its weight in gold if done right.

Take the time now, rack your brain, and tax your resources to figure out how to bring in income immediately to accomplish your vision. Done well, this step brings you into the six-digit income range very quickly.

By the end of 2021, I had achieved 25,000,000 downloads and over 165,000 social media followers.

Daily things-to-do list

The final step of the Vision Map™ is to place actionable items on your list of things to do every day.

This is what you need in front of you at all times.

Sure, you can sleep.

Sure, you can take breaks.

But when you are at work, you need this list in front of you to work on each and every day.

The list is not going to work itself. Even with some team members to help, you still need to be there to organize, control, and direct.

This step appears to be the smallest step and the easiest to understand. Yet, it is this precise step that will encompass some 90% of your time on getting the work done.

It is this step that creates the product, the service, the income, a growing team, and everything else you can think of.

It is this step that creates success, or the lack of this step is what creates failure.

This is the step you must focus on every day if you are serious about that dream you had (your vision).

This step is life and death. There is no playing games with this list. If you and your family want to eat tomorrow, you must focus your life on these steps a majority of the time.

This list grows by the simple means of adding to the list when something else comes up that needs to get done to accomplish your vision. The main items to do today come from your Tactical Plan.

By mid-2020, my fiction book, written with co-author SKR, *Imen of Atlantis: Bitten*, became a bestseller.

The Vision Map™

1. Get your vision in place.
2. Establish your purpose.
3. Set your Long-Term Objective.
4. Work out your Master Plan, including strategic and tactical steps to take.
5. Figure out your 30/60/90 Days of Action to generate immediate income.
6. Determine your shorter-term Things-To-Do List to do each day.
7. Move on that path.

8. Bulldoze obstacles out of your way; keep going!
9. Persist until the Long-Term Objective is accomplished.

Do you think you can do that?

Can you persist regardless of anything and everything?

Can you be the terminator and just keep going and going and going?

Remember this the next time you lose a sale and think that you are nothing or simply worthless.

There is only one thing you can do. Only one. And that is to reach out and talk to more people.

You are to persist no matter the obstacle! By persisting, you will accomplish your short-term actions, which will result in the eventual accomplishment of your Long-Term Objective.

Go back to your Vision Map™, read it over, and act on it again and again. With God's blessings, you'll do great.

By mid-2022, I had achieved 30,000,000 downloads, 200,000 social media followers, and had become the #1 podcast on Chartable worldwide.

About the Author

One of the top podcasts in the country, Tony DUrso interviews those who made it to the top of their category (calling them "Elite Entrepreneurs") and who share their wisdom and advice with the audience.

The Tony DUrso Show is heard every Friday at 2:00 p.m. PST and nationally syndicated on Radio. It's the #1 show on VoiceAmerica and Chartable streaming worldwide.

Breaking the Sound Barrier at 30,000,000 all-time Listens and Downloads, he's a 2x Amazon bestseller and helps millions of entrepreneurs learn from the success of others.

In addition to weekly interviews, Tony's company provides social media marketing to help anyone gain more social media followers and also grow their podcast.

KWE
PUBLISHING, LLC

Starting a Local Community Business

Amy Blain

My background is in television and advertising, and I worked in those fields for twenty-five years. But after working for several companies and dealing with them reducing my commissions, plus their ability to take away clients on their whim, I began to think, *Why am I breaking my back selling ads for these media companies? I should be building my own media property and have something to show for all my years of hard work.*

Meanwhile, the internet happened, and I was fascinated by it. I knew it was going to change the way people did everything, especially shopping and marketing products, services, and events. I wanted to be a part of that because it sounded interesting and challenging. I knew it was going to be the way of the future, and that way I could maybe build my own media empire and profit from that as opposed to working for some company that didn't really care about their clients.

Going off on my own represented freedom for me and the opportunity to do what I am passionate about. Since my background was in events and entertainment, I chose to pursue building a website that helped people find out what was going on in the area.

I started my website, ExplorePeoria.com, because I love helping people figure out what's going on locally. This type of site run by a local entrepreneur is kind of unique.

I work with people like that who are from outside the market, but I also work with a lot of local organizations that are mostly nonprofits, like the community theaters and a lot of other performing arts organizations. I work with some of the festivals, too. We recently shot a video for the Heart of Illinois Fair to help them promote that. We do probably five or six different festivals throughout the year.

One of the other big elements of the business, and it's probably the thing that has brought in the most revenue overall, was building my email list. I started a newsletter shortly after I started the website. All the internet marketers say the money is in the list, and that's definitely the case.

I'm doing it a little differently than they do because I'm doing it on a local level. I'm not asking those individual people who are on my list to buy things from me. It's monetized a little differently than a traditional email list.

Because of my background working at the civic center, I knew that contests were a very effective way to get the word out about events. So, I started doing contests, and once people signed up for the contest, they were automatically subscribed to my newsletter, which is free. That's really what has built my email list over the years, and I continue to run contests today.

I used to put every single event that was on my calendar in my email newsletter, and that could be close to forty events every week. That was a lot, especially as people moved to reading their email on their smartphones with a much smaller screen, so I decided I needed to update the way I handled my newsletter.

Now I do newsletter sponsorships vs. display ads (they were skyscraper ads and were super narrow and difficult to see on a mobile phone). Everybody who is included in my newsletter now is either a paid or trade ad. It's not really an ad; it's actually content marketing. I only include between five and eight events now as opposed to the forty or so I included before. I have a nice big picture of each event, then a line or two of text, and a link to their website or Facebook event page. It's much cleaner and more interesting for my subscribers.

I send the newsletter out every Thursday afternoon, and that's become the main way that I get the information out to people, even more so than the website. People also go to the website, and one of the main features is our big event calendar. So, they'll go and check that out. There are also a lot of people who just get the newsletter, and they'll click on the link to the event calendar to find out what is happening in the area.

The idea with the updated newsletter format is to get people interested in the event so that they want to get more information and click to go to the website or their Facebook page to get all the nitty gritty. I also have a link to my events calendar at the bottom of every newsletter, plus I include links to my current feature articles. It's a lot more user-friendly, especially when viewed on a phone. I think that has made the newsletter even more attractive than it used to be.

That's why we developed our entertainment reports. The interviewees speak straight to the camera so that it feels like they're talking right to the viewer and that makes

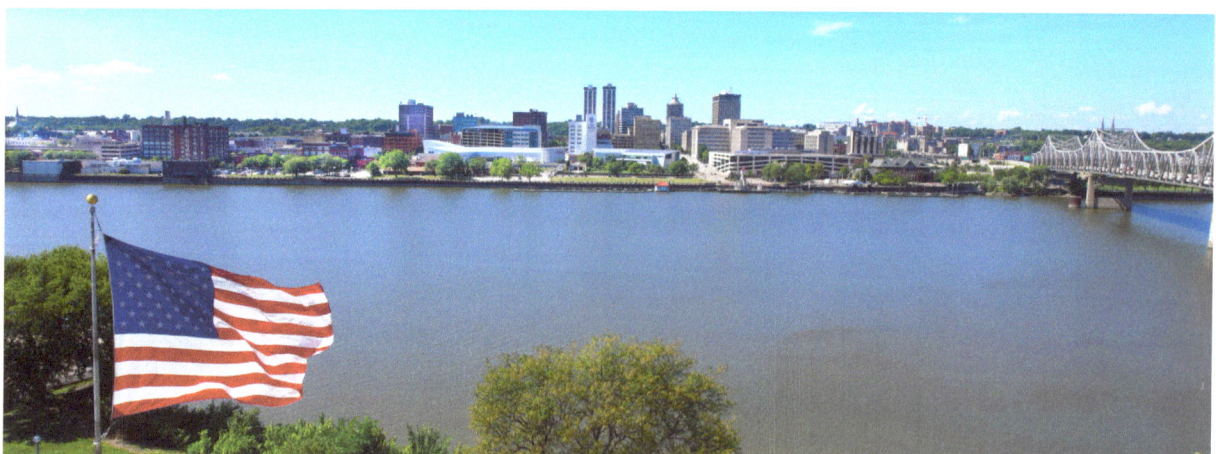

it more personal. It's not like the news; it's more of an infomercial. I would consider it content marketing.

Getting involved in your community depends on the market, but there are all kinds of organizations out there. If you're going to a brand-new community and are looking to meet people and find out what's happening and get involved, I think the best thing to do is to volunteer. There are all types of non-profit organizations that are desperate for volunteers who want to be there and want to make a difference in their community.

This helps those people who you're trying to help, but it also helps you. It is satisfying to know that you're making a difference in your community. It's going to be unique to each area, but there are all kinds of ways to help, and nowadays, there are online forums that can help you get connected.

My best advice for someone starting out in business or building a website like mine is don't do it for the money; do it for the passion. I didn't really know what I was doing at the beginning of it all. I just was kind of taking what I knew, which was media sales, and trying to do my own thing, which I did. At this point, it's probably about as success-ful as it can be.

One of the things I do with my email list is I allow the local event promoters like our museum to send out what I call solo ads, which is essentially an email blast. I only let event promoters do this with my email list because I don't want to have car deal-ers trying to hawk their cars to someone on my list because it's not really "in voice" with what ExplorePeoria.com is about. It's very limited, and the people who are on my subscriber list know that the information in emails from me is all going to be related to events and entertainment.

When I first started ExplorePeoria.com, I had never built a website or anything. I had done TV production, and I'm relatively tech-nical, so I knew I'd figure it out eventually. But initially, it was a little overwhelming.

But as time passed, I got more interested in learning about building my own websites. I really got involved with WordPress, which is what my site is currently built on. It is what a large majority of websites are now built on.

I've become a lot more adept at the technical stuff. I have learned a lot through building my email list and sending emails, working on social media and video, YouTube, and working on other social media platforms. It constantly evolves as you go, and you must keep learning how to do all the stuff that needs to be done.

Making your business financially viable can be tricky. I had experience in media sales, and if I hadn't had that, I would never have been able to make this profitable. And hon-estly, even with that, it took me many years because you have to have something to sell.

It's definitely been a labor of love for me, and it's given me a reason to pursue my interest on the internet and all that has changed over those years since I started. Again, for those wanting to make a lot of money, this may not be the right format, but I know that the nonprofit organizations that I work with appreciate what I've been able to do for them. It's nice to be able to help those orga-nizations and make a difference for them in my local community.

About the Author

Amy has been a seasoned advertising and strategy veteran for over thirty years. She studied mass communication at Illinois State University. She started working at the local NBC affiliate as an intern while in college and later worked there full-time after graduation.

A wife and mom of one daughter and lifelong resident of Peoria, Illinois, Amy has lived in the historical district of Peoria for over thirty years. She has a passion for her local community and neighborhood.

Managing Diversity and Change

Joe Trujillo

As professionals advance in their career fields, they develop a set of managerial characteristics. Within the progression of an occupation, professionals learn to manage themselves, their job selection, and people. The management practices of a person continually reveal their ability to make crucial decisions and lead people in the workplace.

A large portion of making assessments at work comes from interacting with others. Supervising employees requires an understanding of what they are professionally capable of doing and who they are as individuals.

Diversity in the staff of an organization provides workforce versatility and flexibility (Robbins & Hunsaker, 2012). However, being familiar with diversity and knowing it can be useful in a professional environment does not guarantee success for a manager in the workplace.

Diversity is a complex concept of humanity. Part of managing diversity includes utilizing it effectively and comprehending the challenges of those who are faced with it most.

"Diversity is much more than just a multicultural issue. Diversity is about embracing many different types of people, who stand for different things and represent different cultures, generations, ideas, and thinking." (Llopis, 2011, p. 1)

In the pathway to understanding diversity, workforce leaders must realize the modern connotation of the term is far more multifaceted than history has portrayed with race and gender.

Robbins and Hunsaker (2012) describe "inclusive views," factors differing from the traditional dimensions of diversity, and display a large array of human characteristics that have the ability to change over time. (p. 277)

The inclusive views of diversity incorporate the qualities of people, such as personality, lifestyle, and military experience. Llopis (2011) offers the idea that knowledge in Information Technology (IT) has become an aspect of diversity, suggesting a virtual diversity exists in today's workforce.

More than ever, companies are relying on the resources of IT and have comprised entire businesses within the competitive

31

market. The convenience of technology is slowly becoming the standard for the global job market. Advancing IT has allowed professionals to bridge distance gaps and facilitate more efficient ways to conduct business.

Still, understanding the dynamics of diversity remains to be only a feature in the skill of managing it. Managing diversity requires an appropriate application of knowledge to particular groups. In the past, many experts have insisted on positive methods to accept diversity in the workplace, but being sensitive and fair to others is hardly a means of managing diversity.

Anderson (2013) exhibits five steps in the diversity management process: First, ensure all policies, from hiring to promotion, are based on job skill and performance. Second, employ a diverse yet qualified staff of professionals. Third, strive for diversity in team or small group settings. Fourth, take discrimination seriously and enforce a course of action for dealing with such matters. Fifth, periodically hold meetings and training sessions to discuss the benefits of diversity in the workplace.

The steps to managing diversity are ideal suggestions for improving one's leadership skills. Though, after analyzing the process of the five steps, one might avoid thinking about the steps as a sequence. Rather, approach the steps as elements in one's ability to manage diversity.

As businesses attempt to incorporate diversity in a working environment, they face the problems of both sides that are associated. Perhaps the most effective way to manage diversity comes with knowing how to deal with those that are opposed to the concept.

Greenberg (2010) points out three challenges with diversity in the workplace: communication, resistance to change, and implementation of policy. Communication troubles pertain to more than just language barriers but include the interaction of employees and active participation within an organization (or the lack thereof).

Resistance to change often stems from a conservative way of thinking: If it isn't broken, don't fix it. People fear change, and managing this is just as important as anything related to diversity. Implementation of policy breaks the mold of traditional diversity as it becomes more than a way of thinking; it becomes a method of practice for employees.

However managed, there is no denying that diversity exists in the workplace. Fighting the involvement of diversity only seems to limit an individual in their career field. By adopting the positive aspects of diversity into one's managerial skillset, a person adds value to their profession and their practice.

Managing Change

The global workforce is an ever-evolving entity of professional needs and productivity. By facilitating the supply and demand of the business world, workplace leaders must have the managerial ability to implement and supervise change. The management process for change includes planned phases of awareness, employment, and reinforcement. (Robbins & Hunsaker, 2012)

This progression of change requires the use of appropriate skills to be effective, as not all change is welcomed by the working individuals of an establishment. Strategies of controlling and overcoming the resistance to change also allow those in charge to fulfill the necessary adjustments of the workplace.

In a professional environment, it is incumbent upon an establishment to properly incorporate change. "Responsibility for managing change is with management and executives of the organization—they must manage the change in a way that employees can cope with it." (Chapman, 2012)

Making it known throughout the workplace that change implementation is a specific employee's job gives others the opportunity to confide in that person when and if concerns arise. A manager's tasking of change is an obligation that has a significant influence on a company's overall success.

One of the most valuable aspects of a manager's job is in knowing how to lead change. A commonly used method for change is Dr. John Kotter's eight-step process that includes creating a vision, removing obstacles, and following through with achievements. (Kotter international, 2012)

Robbins and Hunsaker (2012) explain these eight steps and also categorize change into three phases: "unfreezing, changing, and refreezing," (p. 237) The unfreezing phase aligns with the vision facet of change. The steps included with this alignment are creating awareness of the need to change, forming a guiding coalition, developing a shared vision, and communicating the vision widely.

These four steps are crucial in the process of change as they assist in making others knowledgeable and eliminating fear. "Lack of information" and "fear of the unknown" are two sources of resistance to change. (Robbins and Hunsaker, 2012, p. 240)

Kotter's attribute of removing "obstacles" couples nicely with the "changing" phase. The steps associated with these moments of workplace transformation are empowering action and generating short-term wins. As a manager arrives at this stage of attaining change, one will begin to notice that these two steps bring their developments to life.

At this point in the process, a manager has created and organized the element of change. By creating change, a manager also has disabled resistance to change by utilizing the strategy of "participation and involvement," which allows those involved to become familiar with the new workplace adjustments. (Robbins and Hunsaker, 2012, p. 241)

The final phase of "refreezing" is paralleled by Kotter's proposed achievement in change. With the last two steps of promoting change, which are evaluating changes and making changes stick, a manager is able to perform a quality check for their implemented alterations. This reassures that the changes have been properly adapted as well as comfortably accepted by those who are affected. Success in this area of change supports the elimination of resistance sources, especially with those such as maintaining "structural stability" and reestablishing "organizational culture." (Robbins and Hunsaker, 2012, p. 241)

In analyzing the initiating steps of change and sources of resistance, a professional can see that the characteristics of the two sides share crossing commonalities. The traits of one step that help create change may also be a strategy for reducing resistance.

For example, step two for promoting change, forming a guiding coalition, is paired best with the strategy of facilitation and support to overcome resistance. Many of the other steps work in the same manner.

Examining further, one may draw a conclusion that the more effective strategy to change is approaching the concept in a less linear process. Instead of looking at the steps to change in chronological order, consider them as a continuing process. Also, with the steps to change thought of as an ongoing sequence, a manager can apply the applicable phases without running through the entire list.

As mentioned earlier, the global workforce is an ever-evolving entity. The effective changes of an organization rely on the proficient skills of a manager to coordinate change. After all, change is the responsibility of every workforce leader.

References

Anderson, A. (2013). How to manage diversity in the workplace. *Chron*. Retrieved from http://smallbusiness.chron.com/manage-diversity-workplace-3038.html

Chapman, A. (2012). *Change management: Organizational and personal change management, process, plans, change management and business development tips*. Retrieved from http://www.businessballs.com/changemanagement.htm

Greenberg, J. (2010). Diversity in the workplace: Benefits, challenges and solutions. *Diversity*.

Retrieved from http://diversity.sdce.edu/content/diversity-workplace-benefits-challenges-and-solutions

Llopis, G. (June 13, 2011). Diversity management is the key to growth: Make it authentic. *Forbes*.

Retrieved from http://www.forbes.com/sites/glennllopis/2011/06/13/diversity-management-is-the-key-to-growth-make-it-authentic/

Kotter International (2012). *The 8-step process for leading change*. Retrieved from http://www.kotterinternational.com/our-principles/changesteps

Robbins, S. P., & Hunsaker, P. L. (2012). *Training in interpersonal skills: TIPS for managing people at work* (6th ed.). Upper Saddle River, NJ: Pearson Education, Inc.

About the Author

Joe is a three-time international bestselling author and three-time bestselling author. He is a competent and performance-driven professional with exceptional procedural skills and a passion for resolving complex problems through innovative solutions.

Joe has a high-leveled aptitude in business administration, process implementation, and project management. With proven leadership abilities in managing diverse work groups, Joe has over twenty years of combined professional experience in operations, communications, manufacturing, and workforce training.

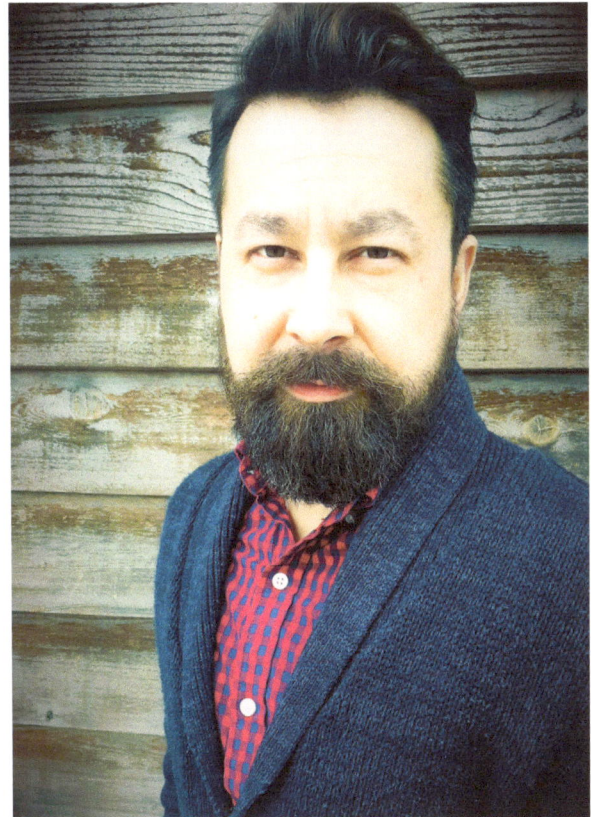

BRIGHT !DEAS MARKETING

Our Clients Have Been Featured On...

PHILADELPHIA BUSINESS JOURNAL   NBC   CBS NEWS   FOX

Pilates for Everyone

Meirav Cohen

> **"** *Take care of your body.*
> *It's the only place you have to live in.* **"**
> **Joseph Pilates**

Many of us think that we need to be strong and flexible to enter a Pilates studio. We hold an image of what a "Pilates body" looks like and how "bad" we would be in Pilates. Some of us think that we need to buy Lululemon tights and crop tops to join a Pilates class, or that we have to be able to hold a plank for one minute. *I am out of shape*, might be a thought that keeps us away or the fact that we haven't exercised since March 2020 due to the global pandemic.

Meirav Cohen, owner of Move With Meirav Pilates Studio, says, "All you need to start a Pilates practice is your body and curiosity."

You don't have to wear fashionable gear, and you don't have to worry about your weight or how you feel about being at home for two years. You don't have to be able to touch your toes when folding forward or stand on one leg for thirty seconds. This Pilates studio is a judgment-free zone. You will be accepted and respected as you are at this point in time and guided through the practice to where you want to be.

Pilates is a physical fitness system developed in the early 20th century by Joseph Pilates. Move with Meirav is a Pilates studio located in the foothills of the Rockies in Boulder Heights. The studio offers private and semi-private instruction.

Meirav is a Colorado transplant, originally from Israel by way of Brooklyn, New York. She has been practicing Pilates since 2009 and teaching since 2012.

Not long after finding Pilates, she began to notice how her movement practice impacted the way she interacted with the world. She felt stronger, more at ease, focused, and confident. She fell in love with Pilates, and later with yoga, earning her yoga teaching certificate in 2019.

Meirav believes, "You can't be good or bad in Pilates; there are no grades or an end-of-the-year performance. Pilates is a promise you make to yourself to take care of your body, a promise to your future self who wants to keep hiking and skiing until old age."

Meirav started her teaching career teaching Pilates in Israel. Shortly after moving

to NYC, she began teaching in several studios. In 2015, Meirav started managing the Pilates studio she was working at in Park Slope, Brooklyn, where she gained a deeper understanding about the business side of the industry.

Meirav enjoys teaching both people who are new to Pilates and advanced practitioners who are seeking ways to challenge their practice. She specializes in teaching pre and postnatal Pilates, supporting moms-to-be and new moms, and has a lot of experience with teaching people recovering from injuries and other physical conditions.

Meirav offers a free thirty-minute intro session where you get to explore if Pilates is for you. In the intro session, you can share your

goals and challenges, plus Meirav will introduce the Pilates apparatus and the studio.

You are not expected to know Pilates, and you are not expected to be flexible or strong. All you need is to show up!

CBD School

Melanie Kossan

My business is called Mountain Mama LLC, and it started out as Mountain Mama Body Butter. I started five years ago, in 2017, making body butters, sugar scrubs, and general self-care products. I was selling them locally at farmer's markets.

It very quickly came to my attention that something was going to have to be different about my product to stand out from the rest. I knew a little about CBD, and after doing more research I began to add it to my products. That was in late 2017.

I was importing full-spectrum CBD distillate from Europe. It was very expensive, and a lot of people didn't know about it, but that was why I was doing it. CBD was what made my product different. It was going to not only be an avenue of self-care because it hydrated the skin and helped you be intentional about self-care, but it also could alleviate some pain and inflammation in your joints and muscles.

I wanted to grow the company. I knew that I wanted to get into stores as a wholesaler, but I had to figure out how. I would have to go to a more progressive area because I knew that Billings wasn't ready.

So, I went west to Bozeman. Not only did people not know what I was selling, but I was kicked out of stores because people's misconceptions caused them to believe that I was trying to convince them to sell something that was illegal in their stores.

At that point, it was around the beginning of 2018, and I knew that education was needed. Education was the key to this industry. So, I created something called CBD School.

I would go to Billings every month and host a seminar. I had a presentation, and people would come and pay to listen to me talk. I would teach them all about cannabinoids: What is CBD? What isn't CBD? How is CBD beneficial in our lives? How can you use it? Why would you use it? And then, in the end, I would have an opportunity for them to buy product. This helped me sell a lot of products, and it was becoming very popular.

I only had twelve seats, and it would sell out every month. I did it for the rest of 2018, and the industry locally began to change. With the signing of the 2018 Farm Bill in December 2017, a lot of other people began doing education as well, and I had some authority because I wasn't just the lone CBD peddler anymore.

People were hearing about CBD from other resources as well, and I was simply providing someplace local where they could go and listen about CBD and ask questions, somewhere they could talk to somebody in person about it.

Additionally, I went on the radio station in Billings every month and did a live question-and-answer session and answered a lot of questions, sold a lot of products, and was able to get into stores. Simultaneously, tinctures were becoming more popular. Customers would come to me and ask if I had tinctures. So, I began to create them. I've always taken customer feedback and customer requests into account when making new products.

I knew that my products needed to be more potent and purer than anybody else's. So, I never did make a 300-milligram or a 600-milligram tincture. I do make a 600-milligram tincture for pets who weigh less than 50 pounds. But since CBD dosing is largely weight based, and no people who were taking CBD weighed less than 50 pounds, I started at 1,000 milligrams or higher.

When you're taking your CBD, you must take it regularly; consistency is key. Making sure you have enough is also key. I've had a lot of people come into my store or my mall kiosk and say, "Oh, I've tried CBD, and it didn't work for me." Inevitably, 100% of the time, if they were willing to try a stronger product like mine, they would always come back and say, "Wow, this was different. This really did help!" And 100% of the time it was because it was a stronger product and had more cannabinoids in it.

Another major difference between Mountain Mama products and many other CBD products is that we have zero THC in ours.

There are a couple of reasons why we stick to zero THC. One is because almost everybody who has a job locally must have a drug test. They either work for the mine, a refinery, drive truck, or something similar, and they must do a DOT test. Many locals are in law enforcement or the medical community, and they must be able to pass a drug test to keep their jobs.

That's a big deal. People will decide whether they'll take a product based on the fact that they have a career that is very important and provides well for their family and provides benefits, and nobody's going to risk that so that they can take CBD.

Once the United States began to grow more and more hemp, the extracts became more widely available in the States. And they were, of course, a lot more cost-effective to buy in the States.

I wanted to buy in Montana because we've always been loyal to locally produced products and made sure to get as many of my supplies and ingredients as I could from my home state. But it took some steps.

At that time, Montana was growing more hemp than any other state in the country. Now, it's Texas. But in the beginning, Montana was leading the pack.

We still have a lot of growers, mainly in the middle of the state, because hemp grows the best in soil where grains grow the best, such as wheat, hay, or alfalfa. They like the same kind of soil. We have something called a golden triangle right in the middle of our state. And that's where most of the country's feed grain is grown.

I am now sourcing all my cannabinoid extract products from one farm in Alberton, Montana. I love this because I think Alberton's population is around 500 people.

In Alberton, there is a 16-acre farm that grows hemp, and they provide all the extracts that we use here at Mountain Mama. They're called Mountain Meadow, and they've been a strong partner with Mountain Mama for years.

We were a match made in heaven. I tried out their product, and I got their lab results and read all their certificates of analysis. After a thorough review, I knew they were putting out a great ingredient, and I wanted to be a part of that.

This year, we also started working with other rare cannabinoids, such as CBG and CBN. There is a lot of great information about rare cannabinoids in CBD School 2.0.

In the last year, we have turned Mountain Mama LLC into a corporation that holds two subsidiaries—a distributorship and a podcast. We've also established the CBD Distributors Association, which is dedicated to education and bringing those in the cannabinoid industry together to form a solid industry infrastructure.

We will always focus heavily on education. We use the podcast for education, both ecommerce websites have blogs on them for education, and the association page is all education. We also offer memberships on the association page. The original CBD School is available online as a free webinar, and CBD School 2.0 is now out.

The distributorship is the vending machine arm where we sell small-business opportunities for people who desire a passive income. We have these great vending machines that are wrapped in a quality brand and come full of product. We have professionals to advise on the placement of the machines, how to sell ads on your machines. Even financing available. It's truly a no-brainer.

Additionally, we do a lot of private labeling. Private labeling is a great way for us to help other businesses be successful. We can make a fantastic product for them, and they can put their own brand on it.

We work with companies who already have a solid following of customers who trust them and value their products and their opinions. When they launch their own CBD line with their label on it, it is always a huge success. It always does very, very well.

We are also working on publishing a print magazine. That will release soon and be published by the CBD Distributors Association. The print magazine will feature others in the cannabinoid industry and how they are benefitting the industry and their communities. This is a great example of other companies supporting other companies in the business community and providing even more education for the consumer.

About the Author

Melanie Kossan is the founder and CEO of Mountain Mama LLC, and a lifelong entrepreneur and natural healthcare advocate. Mountain Mama LLC manufactures many kinds of CBD products and markets to wholesale and private-label clients.

Her brands, stillwaterhemp.com and allnaturaltopicals.com, market these products directly to the consumer via e-commerce and our store fronts. Stillwater Distributors offers a passive income to those who want a piece of the CBD market through a licensed distributorship.

How to Build a Successful Product Brand

Undoubtedly, a good product brand is a major factor in the success of any product. A brand can be defined as an image, personality, or character that consumers identify with. It is the sum of the many elements that make up a product's brand. It is the feeling that people get when they think about a product. It is the reason why people buy a product, and it is the reason why people keep coming back for more. It is how people talk about a product. A brand is a powerful thing.

A brand is more than a logo or name; it is an identity and a promise. Branding is a process that allows a product or service to become synonymous with a particular company or organization. When people think of a certain product or service, they automatically associate it with a specific company, company logo, or a particular name. This association leads them to believe that the product is of a certain quality, which in turn helps to build loyalty and trust among customers.

It is important to build a product brand because it will help you retain customers, create a loyal following, and grow your business. However, there are many things you can do to develop your brand. In this article, we will discuss six ways to build a successful product brand.

1. Define your purpose

Before you begin building a brand, it is important to define your purpose. What does the brand stand for? What are your goals? Why should your target audience care about your product? Are you offering anything new?

Once you have defined your purpose, you can use this information to develop your brand strategy. For instance, if you are trying to sell shoes, you could decide that you want to offer comfortable shoes. You could also decide to promote the benefits of these shoes and provide them at a low cost.

2. Define your audience

Once you know what you want to sell, you need to determine who you want to sell it to. Who are your primary target customers? Your customers are the people who buy your product or service. These are the people who pay for your product and expect you to provide it.

Identifying your audience is an important part of branding. Once you have identified your audience, you can proceed to figure out the needs of this audience. You can learn what your audience wants and what features are most important to them.

3. Understand the competition

Understanding the competition is important to the success of your brand. Do you see yourself as a leader or follower in your market?

There is a difference between being the first and being the best. You should always keep your eyes on the competition. Understanding the competition will help you understand what your customers want and how to improve your product or service.

4. Develop your brand

Once you have determined your purpose, audience, and competition, you can move on to developing your brand. It includes designing a logo, choosing a color palette, creating a tagline, and making sure your design is consistent across all your marketing materials.

5. Find a partner

After you have developed your brand, you will need to find someone to help promote it. This person could be another brand or your existing employees. The person you choose must have the same values and goals as you do.

6. Promote your brand

You've found a partner to help promote your brand; now, you need to find other ways to get the word out about your company. Marketing can be expensive, but there are many free and low-cost ways to get the word out to potential customers.

7. Market your product or service

Once you have a good understanding of your audience and your competition, it's time to market your brand. You can start by advertising on local television, radio, websites, social media, etc. You can also do things like attending trade shows and conventions, putting up flyers in local shops, etc.

8. Track your results

As you develop and market your brand, tracking your results is important. Did your business grow? Why or why not? What did you learn from these results?

9. Start over

It's important to stay on the course and continue marketing your brand. If you've learned anything from your business development, you can incorporate that into your next marketing campaign.

What Are the Benefits of Building A Successful Product Brand?

A product brand is defined as a brand image of a product, company, service, business, or organization. A brand is an impression people get from your product or service.

Branding helps you achieve better results by developing a relationship with your customers, improving your product, service, and business reputation, and creating a distinctive identity that sets your brand apart from others.

Product branding is the process of creating a strong brand image for your product, service, or business. Product branding is the way to develop a distinctive identity that sets your brand apart from others.

Your product or service has a brand, and it's important to define that brand clearly and consistently so that your potential customers recognize it as soon as they see your product or service.

Brands are unique, consistent, and memorable because they are connected with emotions like trust, quality, and value.

Branding is the core part of every business and product. It is the key differentiator between good products and great products.

It is a marketing strategy that focuses on creating a strong identity for your brand and communicating your brand's attributes to potential customers. Let's understand the benefits of product branding:

1. Branding makes your product more credible

Branding is a marketing strategy that builds credibility for your product, service, or company. It helps you establish a trusted reputation and develop a loyal customer base.

When your potential customers see your product or service, they know what they are getting. They can trust your brand and feel confident that you are trustworthy and reliable.

Using a recognizable brand image, you create an association between your brand and your product or service. You build trust, build loyalty, and develop relationships with your customers.

2. Branded products get more sales

Branded products get more sales than non-branded products. Products that are branded by a company are considered more valuable than those with generic labels.

The reason is simple. Customers perceive branded products as more valuable than non-branded products. It increases the chance of higher sales. A study found that companies with strong brands make more sales.

It also found that companies with strong brands have higher gross margins and earn more profit per dollar spent on advertising.

3. Branded products are perceived as better quality

Another study found that people judge the quality of a product more positively when it has a strong brand. People tend to think that if the product has a strong brand, it must be better than the ones with generic labels.

Customers subconsciously expect high quality and value when they see a branded product. They expect that the branded product is going to perform better than the generic product, and they will not hesitate to pay extra money for a branded product.

Studies show that customers will buy a branded product at a higher price than a generic one, even if they are offered a lower price.

4. Stronger brands are easier to sell

A strong brand makes it easier to sell your products or services because people trust it more. For example, consider the Apple iPhone. If you were to go to a store and ask the salesperson for an iPhone, they would probably direct you to a specific model. But, if you had asked them for any smartphone, they would have directed you to the smartphone section of the store. It is because the iPhone brand is so strong that it is easier for the salesperson to point out what a customer can get with the iPhone versus other smartphones.

5. Customer loyalty goes up

People are loyal to their brands and companies. You should never underestimate the power of a brand or company. Your brand is like a promise that you make to your customer. For example, I know that I will always get good service at your fast-food restaurant because you have a brand reputation that says, "We have great customer service." People trust that a fast-food restaurant with a strong brand will take good care of them.

How Can a Successful Product Brand Promote Your Business?

A successful product brand can make the brand of a company or organization visible to the customers. A successful product brand helps you to increase your sales by creating a good image for your brand. Your product brand also influences the customers' perception of your products. So, a successful product brand helps you to promote your business.

There are several factors that influence the success of your product brand. Product branding is a part of the overall marketing strategy. It's important that you use the right strategy for your brand, and the brand should be in sync with the marketing plan.

Product branding is a great way to promote your brand because the product brand is visible to the public. So, people notice your product, and they may ask questions about it. They may even try it. And if they try it, they will become a customer.

Your product brand is visible not only to the public but also to the employees of your company. It will ensure that the employees of your company do not create confusion among the customers by using incorrect labels.

Your product brand should have a unique identity. It will help your customers remember your brand. You can keep your brand identity simple or complicated, depending on the type of product you sell.

Additional Tips to Help You With Building A Successful Product Brand

Here are a few tips to help you with building a successful product brand.

1. Have a vision

You should have a vision for your product brand. What do you want your product to be like? What is your target market? Where do you want to take your brand?

It is the first step to success. You must know what you want.

2. Choose a name

Choose a name that matches your vision. When choosing a name, make sure it has nothing to do with anything else and is unique.

Make sure that the name you choose is catchy and memorable.

3. Choose a logo

Now that you have chosen a name, you need to create a logo for your brand. It is one of the most important parts of your product brand. You should start by choosing a design theme that matches your product. Once you have a design, you need to have a designer create a logo for you.

4. Create a website

A website will give you a platform to spread the word about your brand. Make sure that your website has a logo and a strong design. A good website will encourage people to sign up for your newsletter or subscribe to your social media accounts. You also want to make sure that your website has a clear call-to-action button.

5. Build trust

People will buy your product because they believe in you. Make sure that your customers know who you are and why they should trust you. Make sure you use testimonials and reviews on your website. Your website should look professional and trustworthy.

6. Testimonials

You want to build trust with your customers. Tell your customers how great your product is. Make sure you offer discounts and free shipping.

7. Customer Service

If you want to have a successful product brand, then you need to take care of your customers. Make sure that your customers know that you care and that you want them to be happy with your product.

You should answer all emails within 24 hours. You should also reply to comments on your social media accounts. Good customer service can go a long way.

8. Promote your products

Promoting your product is one of the most important things. You want to make sure that your customers know about your product.

Share your promotions on Facebook, Instagram, Twitter, Pinterest, and other social media platforms.

Top 7 Rules of Building A Successful Product Brand

To build a successful brand, you need to follow some rules. Here, we present you with the top 7 rules that will help you to make your product brand a huge success.

Rule 1: Find your product's niche market

The first step to building a successful brand is to find out what your customers want and how they want it. By understanding your product's niche, you'll be able to design a product that meets the exact needs of your targeted audience.

Rule 2: Create a clear vision for your product

A product's brand needs to be unique. Your brand shouldn't sound like any other similar product. If you do not create a clear vision for your product, you might end up designing something that sounds cool but doesn't meet your needs. When creating a vision for your product, keep in mind that it should be simple, clear, and easy to understand.

Rule 3: Use visual design tools and resources

Designing a successful product requires using the right tool. Tools such as Sketch, Figma, or Invision can help you in creating a successful design. Design tools can help you quickly create a unique visual design for your product.

Rule 4: Create a consistent product name

Product names play a vital role in developing a successful brand. When creating a product name, keep in mind that it should be catchy and meaningful. In addition to this, your product name should be simple, short, and unique.

Rule 5: Create a memorable logo

Your logo is the most visible part of your product brand. A good logo represents your product's uniqueness. You can use a variety of techniques to create a memorable logo.

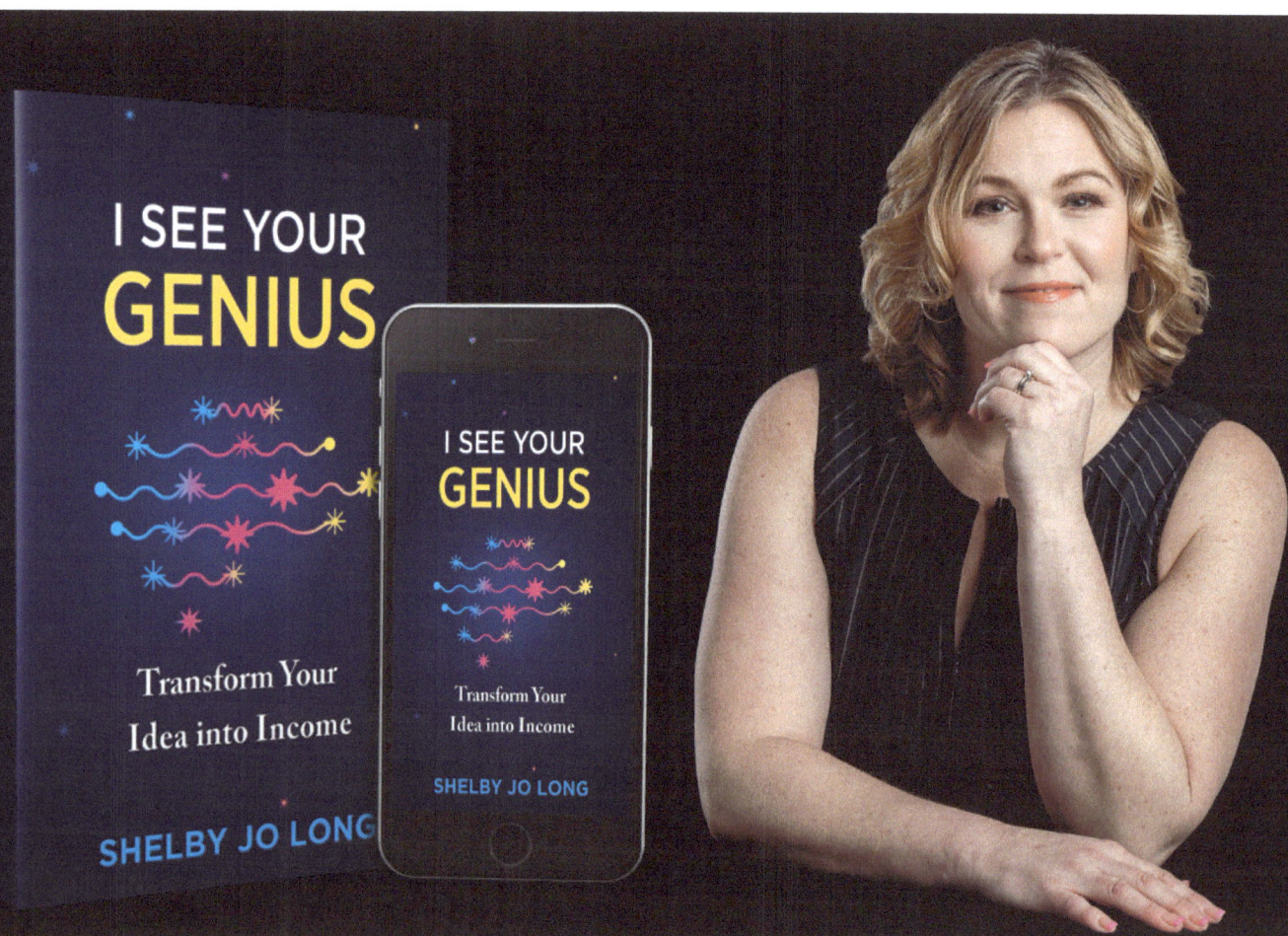

For instance, you can create a logo using icons, shapes, or a combination of both.

Rule 6: Use social media marketing

Social media marketing is one of the best ways to build your brand. Social media platforms are the perfect place to get the word out about your product. Once you launch your product, make sure to use social media channels to promote your brand.

Rule 7: Give feedback on the reviews

Feedback is extremely important to the development of a successful product. You should provide feedback to your customers once they review your product. It will help you to identify the areas in which your product could use improvement.

In conclusion, to build a successful product brand, you need to focus on your product's benefits, how to use it, how to get more people to use it, and how to get more people to recommend it to their friends.

Advertisers

www.ingramcontent.com/pod-product-compliance
Lightning Source LLC
Chambersburg PA
CBHW041452210326
41599CB00004B/229